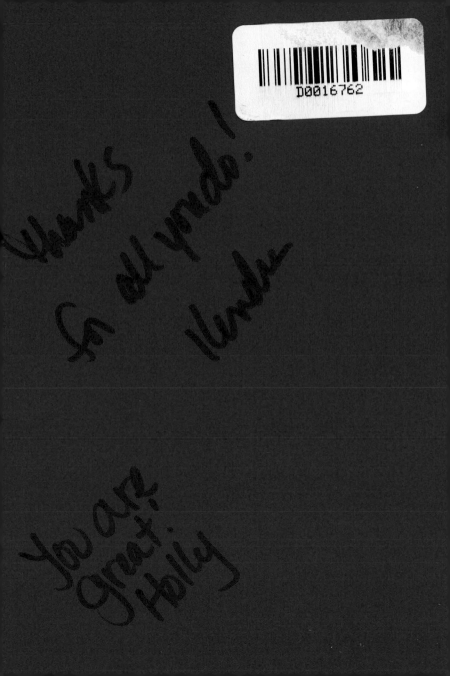

thanks
So all you do!

Hendrix

You are
great.
Holly

D0016762

The **Ball**

TODD WHITAKER

TRIPLE
NICKEL
PRESS

555 North Morton Street
Bloomington, IN 47404
888.369.3179
FAX: 812.336.7790
email: info@triplenickelpress.com
triplenickelpress.com
Printed in the United States of America
14 13 12 11 10   1 2 3 4 5

FSC

Mixed Sources
Product group from well-managed
forests, controlled sources and
recycled wood or fibre

Cert no. SW-COC-002673
www.fsc.org
© 1996 Forest Stewardship Council

Library of Congress Control Number: 2010930417

The only behavior
we can change
is our own.

About the **Author**

Todd Whitaker has been fortunate to be able to blend his passion with his profession. A leading presenter in the fields of education and leadership, his message has resonated with over a million professionals around the world. One of the nation's leading authorities on employee motivation and leadership effectiveness, Whitaker has written over twenty books and has been invited to present in all fifty states and numerous countries around the world. He is a professor of educational leadership at Indiana State University in Terre Haute, Indiana. Todd and his wife, Beth, also a professor at Indiana State University, have three children: Katherine, Madeline, and Harrison.

The **Ball**

Annie Erickson woke up a little earlier than usual

that autumn day—

well before her alarm sounded. She sang in the shower and while she dried her hair. It was cupcake day; for the first time in many years, it was cupcake day again.

When she thought back over the twenty years she'd taught fifth graders, she could remember a time when she sprang from bed *every* morning to get to work—when she couldn't wait to get there, when it was a thrill each time her students finished a special unit or accomplished something extraordinary. In those days, she brought cupcakes to celebrate their achievement. But time and changes took their toll, and eventually, she abandoned the cupcake tradition, like so many others. She was still "Miss E." to her students, but something was missing. So this year, her twentieth,

4

Miss E. decided to renew the cupcake tradition.

Annie almost skipped to her car as she thought about the stop she was going to make on the way to work. Just as she used to years ago, she was going to CF Market, a locally owned grocery known for its striped colorful awning, superior produce, and delicious baked goods. She hadn't been there since she moved to the other side of town ten years ago, but she remembered its fresh smells, smiling faces, and just-cleaned look. She hummed to herself in anticipation as she drove.

When she pulled into the lot, **Annie** Though it was early in the morning, the parking lot was littered with carts. The landscaping was overgrown and weedy, the faded awning sagged on one side, and the windows were streaked with grime. She had heard some rumors that the market had changed, but she had no idea it was so far gone.

When she used to shop at CF Market regularly, the owner, Mr. Fulton, was one of the most customer-friendly and dedicated

was stunned
by what she saw.

owners she had ever known. She had had the pleasure of teaching his son Billy in one of her first classes—in fact, Billy was one of her all-time favorite students—and Mr. Fulton used to chat about his son's school-work whenever she was in the market. He would never have let the store deteriorate.

Though she was saddened by the market's condition, Miss Erickson's resolve to reward her students was undaunted. She was glad she'd left home early—the building's appearance suggested that the store might not major in efficiency—but there was still time to save cupcake day. She headed straight to the bakery to pick up two dozen cupcakes for her students and a cup of coffee for herself.

The bakery didn't look like Annie remembered it.

No seasonally decorated cookies were on display, no aroma of fresh bread wafted through the aisles, and the counter where she used to get a cup of fresh hot coffee appeared

shut down. The lone employee behind the counter was tagging prepackaged rolls with "reduced" stickers—and working diligently at not making eye contact. She waited for what seemed like an eternity, trying to put herself in his line of vision. Finally, after she cleared her throat politely several times, the clerk grunted, "Yeah?"

Annie knew right then that Mr. Fulton no longer owned the store. Never would one of his employees have spoken to a customer like that. In his day, there were always half a dozen people eager to serve in every part of the store.

Having finally gotten some attention, she asked, "Could I please have twenty-five cupcakes?"

The clerk motioned over to a shelf that displayed some less-than-impressive baked goods. "There's some muffins," he said, "but the cupcakes are still in back. They're not frosted yet."

"Hmm," Miss Erickson said. "I really wanted cupcakes. Do you think you could frost them for me while I wait?"

The clerk sighed and jabbed another sticker on another package of rolls. "Fiiine," he droned, "but it's gonna be a while."

Annie was taken aback, but **she was determined that nothing today was going to dampen her spirit.** Just then she turned around and almost ran directly into a man in a shirt and tie. His head was down and his shoulders slumped, but even so, she recognized him instantly. "Billy, Billy Fulton!" she cried happily, grasping his arm. She appraised his height. "Of course, you're probably not 'Billy' anymore, are you?"

Bill hesitated, then slowly his furrowed brow relaxed. "Miss E.? Is that really you? Wow, it *is* you!" He laughed, and they hugged briefly. "What are you doing here?"

Annie explained that she was renewing a classroom tradition that she had let drop: she was taking cupcakes for her students to celebrate the end of a special unit. Bill lit up.

"I remember when you used to do that for us," he said. "We loved it! Do you still put the little trinkets in the frosting?"

"I'm hoping to," Miss E. replied, "the students will be so thrilled. But the young man in the bakery . . . Well, it seems like it may take quite a while to frost two dozen."

"Let me see if I can help," Bill said.

Annie gave him a puzzled look. He smiled and tapped his pocket, where a name-tag read "Bill Fulton, Manager/Owner."

Once he got behind the counter with the clerk, however, Bill's smile vanished and his voice rose. "For crying out loud, Ricky, aren't you done with that stickering yet?" he demanded. "What's the matter with you? Get to it! She doesn't have all day."

After his outburst, Bill rejoined Annie in the aisle. "That clerk will get to work on

Can't you see the customer is waiting?

The room

the cupcakes right now," he said. He was flushed and seemed a little embarrassed. "Listen, Miss E., do you have a few minutes to catch up?"

She heard sadness in his voice. She studied Bill and thought how tired he looked. He had the same blue eyes and full head of hair he'd had as a boy, but today, he looked worn out and worn down. She put her hand on his arm and squeezed it. "I'd love to visit," she said.

Bill led her back to the worker break room, where three employees were clustered, talking in low voices; they stopped talking and scattered when Bill opened the door.

had a terrible musty smell.

Two of the fluorescent lightbulbs flickered,

and one of the walls was literally covered with handwritten signs, sticky notes, and memos. Some looked like they had been there for many years, with yellowed tape and faded ink; others had vigorously circled or underlined text that looked recent.

They sat down at a wobbly table. "Tell me, how long have you worked here?" Annie asked.

"Off and on ever since I was a little boy," Bill said. "My grandfather built this market. When he retired and moved away, my dad took over, but his health failed about six years ago. So I came back to town to keep the family business alive." He sighed. "But unfortunately, it looks like the business is about to die. Unless things turn around, I'm afraid I'll have to shutter the grocery store at the end of the year."

"Oh, no," said Annie. "That's so sad."

"It sure is. When I took over, this was a thriving business, but about five years ago, business really dropped off." Bill rubbed his forehead. "Honestly,

I'm at the

end
of my rope.

I've laid off employees,

stopped almost all
staff benefits,

limited the products we order . . ." He shrugged. "But even though I've fought to cut every possible penny in costs,

I still can't
make ends meet.

"The big box stores, the StuffMarts, and the giant grocery chains—how can I compete with them? They're killing small businesses like mine, businesses that have been around for years. I don't know how I'll tell my father if I have to close the store." His voice cracked.

Miss E. had always been a great listener, but Bill was still embarrassed to share his struggles. He straightened in his chair.

"Well, enough of that. Tell me more about you and your life. What made you want to bring back your cupcake tradition?"

Annie hesitated, but Bill didn't seem willing to talk further about his situation at the store. She reflected for a moment to gather her thoughts.

"When I first started teaching," she began, "I loved coming to school every day. Every aspect of my work was fun. I especially loved teaching students about life, and I tried to bring that into the classroom whenever I could. We had some wonderful lessons.

"But the best part of the day for me didn't take place in the classroom at all.

It was recess!

It wasn't that I wanted a break from teaching. I just loved going outside with the children to play. Whether it was hopscotch, kickball, or softball, I loved interacting with my students casually." She smiled, reminiscing. "Of all the games, my favorite was four square."

"Mine, too!" Bill said. "I remember how we would line up by the painted squares on the playground to see if we could beat the current champion."

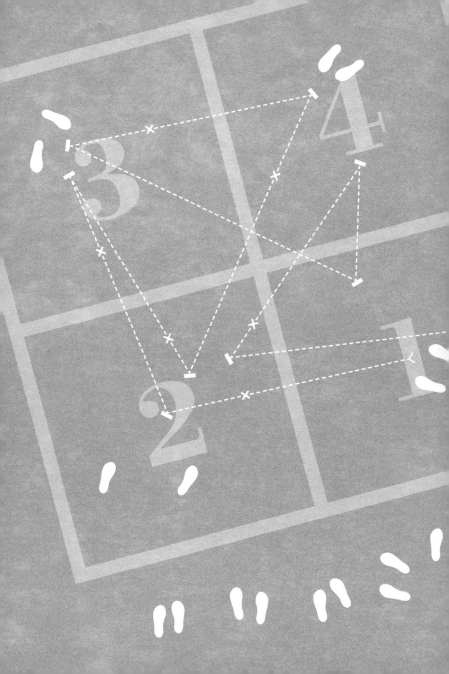

"That's right, you did. And through all those games," Annie went on, "I taught many of life's lessons to my students. They learned to take turns, do their best, be honest, work well together, follow rules. . . . So many lessons, and we all had so much fun together."

"You were a great teacher, Miss E. So what changed?"

"I don't know." Annie took a deep breath. "Actually, I think it all started when our administration changed. The new principal meant well, but—well, for example, when one of the big neighboring schools started a special program on health education, he sent a memo that we needed to offer a program like that, too. It seemed important to him, so I stayed inside one day a week to plan for that new mandate.

"Then the state handed down mandates for grade-level testing, so I cut going out for recess down to twice a week. Then the school board wanted a day for drug education, and then we were emailed a new directive for a student money-management unit. All of these things, of course, were important at the time, though many of them have fallen by the wayside or were replaced by new marching orders. Anyway, I was working harder and harder to try and meet all the mandates, and **gradually, I just gave up the time at recess with the children, even though I loved it so much.**

Bill seized her arm. "I know exactly what you mean! I always loved working here as a teenager, and when I took over the family store, I really wanted to do the right thing, so I joined a grocers association to learn more about the business. They have new memos at least once a week about what we should be doing, and I go and visit our enormous competitors, and then I come back here and try to imitate what they do to succeed . . ." His voice trailed off. "But the job's not fun anymore

36

and honestly, the new 'improvements' seem to make things worse." He paused. "So are you back on the playground at recess now?"

Annie nodded. "Definitely! I don't recall the exact day, but at the end of last year,

I started noticing how

unhappy

my students were

They no longer worked together, they didn't take turns, and they seldom did their best independently. They just seemed to lack loyalty to each other, to the class, or to the school—"

Nothing

"That sounds just like my employees!" Bill said, smacking the table with his hand. "If you can call them that." He shook his head. "It must be society today. Surely that's the reason things seem to be falling apart, right? Well, that's spilt milk, isn't it? **we can do about it now.**"

He sighed, "Anyhow, I got you off track. . . . So what happened then?"

"Well," Annie said, "I looked out one day during recess, and I saw the four-square game just sitting empty with one of the old red rubber balls resting in the painted grid. And then it came to me."

She leaned forward. "The problem was I had

I let someone else tell me what was important, and I lost sight of what mattered most, what really mattered, to *me*.

"Of course, all of the basic skills we are required to cover are important, and no one can argue with health education, drug education, and so on, but sometimes we have to make a stand for the things that make our work personally meaningful." She looked into Bill's eyes. "I decided to take a stand.

"The very next morning I announced to my students that we were going to start

taken my
eye off of
the ball."

having four-square tournaments every day at recess. I explained the rules of the game and that we were going to play as a class. The kids were puzzled, but I just asked them to give it a try for the rest of the week.

"When our morning break came, we marched outside, and I drew some names out of a can to form teams. At first, the students who weren't chosen rolled their eyes, but I explained everyone would get a turn. The first few days were a little rough, but gradually they learned to love it." She smiled conspiratorially. "And little did they know, I was also teaching them how to take turns, do their best, be honest, work well together, learn to follow rules, and many other life lessons.

The main thing is that class became fun again — outside and inside the classroom."

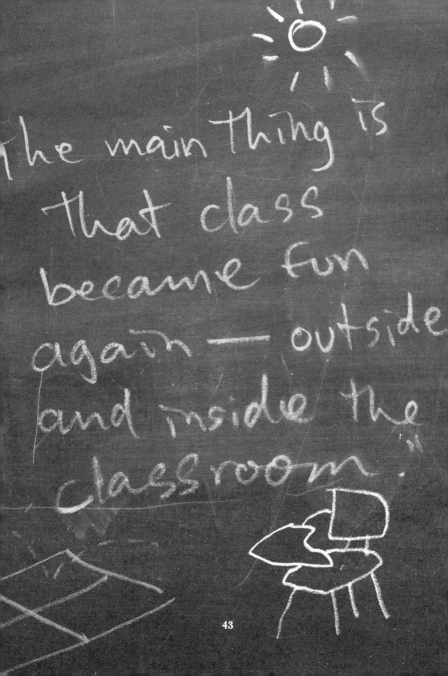

Bill nodded enthusiastically. "I loved four square. In fact, I remember how much we *all* loved it. We didn't realize everything you were teaching us, but we sure did work together as a class. Now I see why it was so important." He raised his hand. "But wait a minute—what does this have to do with the cupcakes?"

"Well, one of the other memos I received from the new administration was about how students are too fat and the school is at fault, so we needed to stop giving them sweets. I had given up so many of my traditions by then that I just threw in the towel completely. I used to give cupcakes several times a year on special occasions, but that memo was the last straw. I just quit the cupcake tradition altogether.

no more games
no more treats
no more fun

45

I was AMBUSHED all the

"That's a shame," Bill said. "We felt so special on those days when you brought us cupcakes. They always had a little trinket on top—I remember I saved all of mine in a little box—and you would tell us about the trinket and how it had a hidden meaning or lesson for us. One time it was a plastic mirror—what was that lesson?" He thought for a minute. "Oh right,

be true

to yourself.

That's ironic, isn't it? I could sure use that lesson again these days."

"You know what, for several years I could have used that lesson, too," Annie said quietly, "but now I am full speed ahead. Because here's what I've realized:

if I'm not true
to myself,

I can't be there
for **anyone** else,
either."

Bill nodded, and they smiled at each
other for a moment.

Miss E. broke the silence by gesturing at the eyesore next to them: "All right, now tell me about your wall covered with paper!"

Bill groaned.

"This wall is a perfect

IF the

chatter

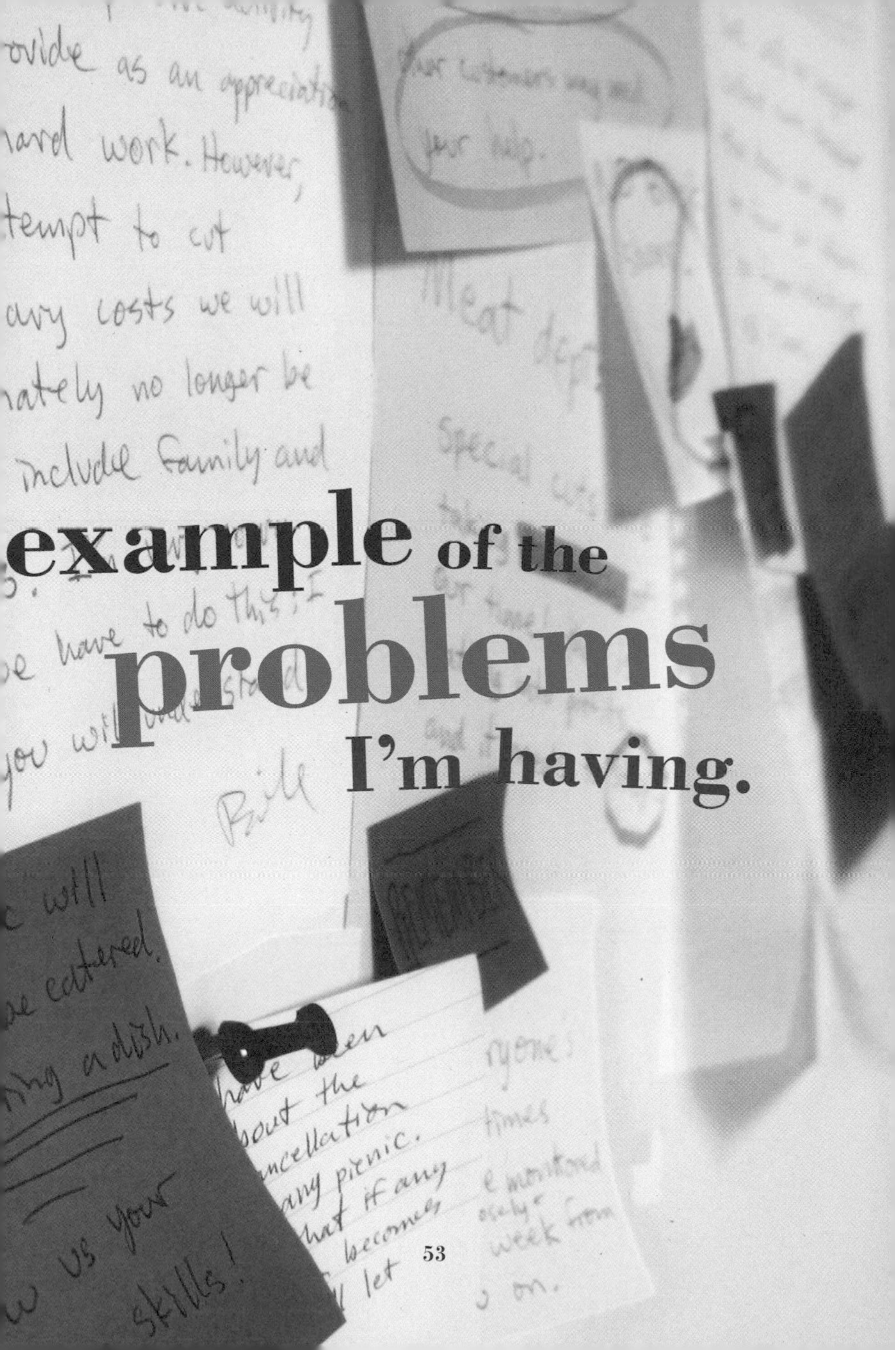

example of the problems I'm having.

I tell my employees to do something, and they do it only halfheartedly at best. And since we've lost so many customers, I have to keep demanding more and more from staff, and reinforcing the new policies. But it doesn't seem to work. **They still** just

Miss E. reached up and pulled a piece of paper off the wall. "What's this one?"

Bill half laughed. "One of our customers —ex-customers, I mean—Mrs. Johnson, used to come in all of the time, and she always wanted the meat department to prepare all these special cuts for her.

"I told our butcher to stop doing that because we couldn't make enough profit on his time, but he kept cutting special orders for her anyway. Finally I made a rule and put it up on this wall."

don't seem to care."

"Here's another example." He pulled off a full-sheet memo, which instructed employees to stop gathering carts each hour and to do it only once a day to save money. **Then he grabbed a sticky note that read,**

We can no longer help customers carry out groceries. We can't afford the employee time that it takes.

He shook his head.

"You know, we even used to deliver groceries to people's homes. We were losing money hand over fist with that."

Bill went through a dozen examples and then turned to Annie. "See why I'm so frustrated? We used to do a lot of things that I've had to put a stop to, to try and get my staff focused on our core business. That's what the big chains do. They're not

getting nickel and dimed to death on the details." He crumpled up the memo about special-order cuts of meat and threw it aside in disgust.

Annie looked at the wad of trash on the floor for a moment, then met Bill's eyes. "Actually, Bill, I happen to know Mrs. Johnson. She lives in my neighborhood. I remember that she mentioned that she used to come here all of the time and then started going to one of the grocery chains."

"See what I mean?" Bill interjected. "Those big stores are killing me."

"Well, she told me that it was much handier for her to come to CF Market," Annie said, "and she loved the personal service. She quit because the big store was cheaper and **you didn't offer the personal experience** anymore, **not even at a higher price.** The big store was even willing to cut those special lamb chops for her. It wasn't everything she wanted—it wasn't local— but it was more than she was getting here.

"And I hate to tell you this, Bill, but the teacher whose room is next to mine, Maria Rodriguez, also used to shop here. Your dad would deliver to her aunt who lived alone and couldn't drive anymore. Maria knew it was more expensive here, but she always said that **if CF Market can go out of the way for her aunt, she will go out of the way for CF Market.** I'm afraid I've heard many other stories like this." She gave him a rueful look.

"By the way," Annie added, "what about the big bold handwritten sign right in the middle of the wall—the one that says,

EMP

PIC

CA

off.

That looks like a new sign. What happened?"

Bill sighed. "Well, the annual picnic was a big tradition that everyone loved, including me, but when I took over about five years ago, we had to start cutting costs. I didn't want to cut salaries or services, so I trimmed some nonessentials, like one of the independent grocer newsletters suggested. The picnic was a huge catered event, and not cheap, so a few years ago, we tried making it employees only—no more family members—to save money. That didn't go over well, so last year, we made it a potluck. I thought maybe that would save money *and* rekindle some team spirit, but hardly anyone came. Yesterday, I started thinking about going through the picnic hassle again and got so mad that I just called it off. I feel bad about it. I don't know what to do. People complained when we had it, people complained when I cancelled it. I can't win!"

Annie tilted her head. "Remind me: what are you trying to win? You know, when I reintroduced our four-square game, some of the students would taunt the others after they lost. Others would mope around for hours after they'd lost, complaining that the rules were unfair or claiming someone had cheated. One of the lessons we had to talk about is that we don't play to win or lose a single game.

It's about playing the game

Or at least that's what I teach my students— to have fun playing the game, today and tomorrow." She studied the wall of memos.

Abruptly she said, "There's something else I've been meaning to ask. Was your grandfather's first name Charles?"

"No, why?"

the right way,
and having
fun doing it.

"I just assumed that is what the 'CF' stood for in CF Market—Charles Fulton."

Bill shook his head, half smiled, started to reply, and then there was a sudden jolt as the bakery employee swung open the door and announced, "Those cupcakes are done."

Annie thanked him politely and noticed that Bill had started ripping the rest of the

memos and sticky notes off the wall. She glanced at her watch and realized that she needed to go. She told Bill she needed to leave for school, and he offered to carry the cupcakes out to her car. As he placed the box of cupcakes on the backseat, he asked her, "So tell me, Miss E., what's the trinket this time for your frosted goodies?"

"I'm glad you reminded me!" she said. "I still need to put them on the cupcakes. You know, I even have one extra cupcake that I was going to eat myself, but I would rather give it to you." She took a cupcake out of the box, reached into her purse, and pulled out a bag. In a moment she turned and handed him the extra treat. **In the middle of the frosting, she had gently placed a round, red ball.**

"Here you go, Bill," she said. "Today's lesson is making sure you never take your eye off of the ball. I think all of us need a reminder about that at times."

Bill studied the cupcake for a moment, took a deep breath, and nodded. "You're right. I need to remember what's really important. I need to remember the lessons of my grandfather and father—to remember the lessons I learned from you, Miss E., about making people feel special." He hugged her. "How can I teach my employees the lessons that I learned from you?"

Miss Erickson pulled back from the hug, paused, smiled, and reminded him,

"Well, you have a bakery, don't you?"

She patted him on the shoulder, got into her car, and drove off.

Bill walked back into the break room and stood there for a moment, thinking. Then he went to the storage closet, got out a ladder, and changed the flickering lightbulbs. Next, he pulled off all the remaining memos and flyers. He stepped back and looked at the newly revealed wall. Underneath all the memos, the wall was painted with a big red circle that looked like an old playground ball.

Two words stood out in the middle, with huge first initials:

Customers First

In the weeks following her visit to the market, Annie remembered her conversation with Bill. She made it a point to drive by the store every day, and over time, she noticed that things were

changing. After that day, the carts were always neatly gathered. Within a few days, the awning was replaced and the windows cleaned. Soon, the parking lot was filled up quite regularly with cars.

One day, Miss E. parked there herself, and went inside to pick up a new order of cupcakes. At the bakery counter, the clerk looked up and smiled. He politely asked, "How can I help you today, ma'am?"

Over his shoulder, she could see a handwritten notice posted to all of the employees:

Company Picnic

THIS SATURDAY!

Bring your families

Four-square tournament.

o FREE FOOD o

Cupcakes for dessert.

Readers' Guide

The Ball tells the story of a declining business from the perspectives of the new owner, Bill, and a former customer, Annie, who happens to be his former teacher. Together, they explore what went wrong, and how to make it right again. The following questions may be used for reflection on the lesson of *The Ball* and how to apply that lesson to your professional and personal life.

Professional Reflection

1. The cupcake lesson is to never take your eye off the ball. What is "the ball" in this story? In your organization?

2. Has your organization taken its eye off of the ball? If so, how can you regain your focus?

3. Is it realistic to still put customers first? Who are your customers?

4. In what way do you make your employees feel special? Would they agree with your answer?

5. In the story, Annie explains that she stops playing with her students at recess in order to address new initiatives—initiatives that were later dropped or downgraded from urgent. What are some initiatives that have come and gone in your organization? Does this hurt employee buy-in when new ideas arise?

6. Do you believe that customers are willing to pay more for better service, a different environment, or other "extras"? How can a business determine whether its extras are of value to customers or simply lost profit?

7. Explain the connections among employee morale, customer service, and financial success that the story suggests.

8. When Annie says she decided to take a stand, what does she mean?

9. Why are celebrations like the cupcakes and employee picnic important? How do you

celebrate in your organization? How should you celebrate in your organization?

10. Annie tells Bill, "We don't play to win or lose a single game. It's about playing the game the right way, and having fun doing it." What does she mean by that?

Personal Reflection

1. In your personal life, what is your "ball"?

2. Have you taken your eye off what's important? If so, how can you regain your focus?

3. What can you do to balance the need to focus on the ball with the other priorities in your life?

4. Are there traditions in your own life and family that you have given up? What are they? Should you consider renewing any of them? How can you bring back important lost traditions?

5. How do you juggle the balls between your personal life and your professional life? What changes would you like to make, if any?

COMPOSED IN CHAPARRAL AND BODONI
CHAPARRAL WAS DESIGNED BY CAROL TWOMBLY IN 1997 AND
NAMED FOR THE CHAPARRO OAK LANDS OF CALIFORNIA
BODONI IS BASED ON THE TYPEFACES OF ·
GIAMBATTISTA BODONI (1740–1813)

PRINTED ON UNCOATED 100% POST-CONSUMER
RECYCLED PAPER MADE WITH WIND POWER
GREEN SEAL AND FSC CERTIFIED

PRINTED BY THOMSON-SHORE ON A HEIDELBERG SM 102
USING SOY-BASED INKS